THUG

THUG

Two Tales
in
Poésie Noire

David Jonathan Jones

2019

THUG

I

The rain falls like nails,
Hammering the asphalt clean,
Glistening the night.

A brief, cool respite,
A kiss blown at a tumour,
A forlorn gesture.

The rain is a lie,
It washes over us all
But changes nothing.

I huddle armoured,
Hat, overcoat, revolver,
I'm impregnable.

Empty street, crossroad,
The Brownstone looms large, solid,
A mausoleum.

I wait for my cue,
A second-floor light goes out,
I wait in the rain.

I give half an hour,
Cross the road to the dun tomb,
The lock gives easy.

Darkness, up two floors,
Outside his door I listen,
Just the rain outside.

Another lock gives,
Inside, dark, I hear him snore,
I cross to the bed.

Half lit his bulk stirs,
Smells, whisky, cigarettes, sweat,
Eyes open startled.

His voice, scared "Hey wait!"
I strike, the gun breaks his mouth,
Nothing I need hear.

Radio dial, on,
Soft jazz floods the slaughterhouse,
I strike again, hard.

Slumped, bloody, out cold,
I wipe my piece, holster it,
Its job done for now.

I take out the scarf,
Cool silk, her perfume clinging,
It slips round his neck.

I pull, he comes to,
Urgent fingers at the noose,
I pull tighter still.

Gurgles, blood, spit, piss,
He slips back into the nod,
I offer him up.

The final twitches,
I snake the silk from off him,
Turn off the music.

Leave, I see no one,
Invisible, just a guy
Out in the damn rain.

The car, radio,
Night voices and soft bebop,
A blood requiem.

Slow drive in the rain,
Park, stairs, my room, could be his,
No strangled fatman.

Slip my hat and coat,
Drape the silk over the bronze,
Her four arms catch it.

I touch cold metal,
Words, red candy at her feet,
I've given enough.

I sit on the bed,
Nightstand, scotch, pour three fingers,
First slug, that good burn.

I take off my gun,
Blue steel close on the bedpost,
Loaded, all options.

Turn the dial, music,
Something shrill, aching, mournful,
It fits like a glove.

I open the draw,
Ampoules, syringe, rubber tube,
I take out the goods.

Snap the glass, draw up,
I noose the tube round my arm,
Tight, I find a vein.

Needle, blood plume, push,
A slow bomb of pleasure bursts,
I disintegrate.

II

Yellow, white and red.

Brains. Bone, blood in pools and sprays,

A holdup gone wrong.

Two very dead men,

A fat liquor store owner,

A stick-thin robber.

Both had a shotgun,

Sawed off twelve gauges times two,

Neither has a face.

No one saw the heist,

There were shouts, then a twin beat,

They shot together.

"What a fucking mess!"

"A day at the office, Jim."

Johnson grins and nods.

The store smells of meat,
There's nothing to be done here,
This case is closed tight.

I leave him to it.
Quizzing the dead for I.D.
I need noise and booze.

I scope a few joints,
Drift on waves of scotch and jazz,
Let my thoughts wander.

I try and detach,
Responsible, a big word,
Can't shift the cop mask.

A cop told me once,
"That badge is a ton of lead."
It's a weight tonight.

Each drop of blood spilled,
Every scream in the night,
Somehow, it's my fault.

My wife's leaving words:
"You carry this city's guilt!"
She ditched the burden.

Focus on street noise,
Scotch and traffic jamming hard.
My footsteps, the beat.

I up the tempo,
Ragged breath, blood sings, a door,
I am in a bar.

III

This place, below dive,
Bebop, dark, sweet-sick tea smoke,
Nothing in focus.

Her, on a cushion,
Like a cat cleaning itself,
Her, oblivious.

Skin, luminous dark,
Axe like nothing of this world,
Those still, ancient eyes.

Like nothing I'd seen,
Exotic beyond foreign,
Even in this hell.

A sound from some dream,
A long, insane instrument,
An angel's guitar.

The combo spun beats,
And she laid heaven on this,
With a cat-slick ease.

Her set finishes,
Ragged claps, the crowd drunk, stoned,
Her pearls before swine.

She cases her axe,
Coffin for a sideshow freak,
Picks it up, heads out.

The drunk grabs her arm,
"What kind of nigger are ya?"
Calm hate in her eyes.

"Or is ya a Mex?"
He turns to the crowd laughing,
Only me watching.

I want to break him,
Tear the drunk eyes from his head,
Piss in the sockets.

She is strange beauty,
In the grip of human shit,
Anger, guilt, I move.

She smiles at the drunk,
He leers back "How much baby?
All cunt got a price!"

Before I reach her
The case smashes his groin hard,
He drops like a stone.

He screams, "Fucking bitch!"
She cats away from his lunge,
I'm in front of him.

"Leave the lady be."
"What's the spick whore to you, man?"
"Leave the lady be."

He stinks of cheap hood,
Shoes, rings, suit louder than war,
Mouth like a sewer.

"Know who I am, fuck?"
"You're just shit to me, buddy."
He claws under cloth.

A glint of blue steel,
I kick him fast in the throat
And pick up his gun.

"Time for bed, asshole!"
On his knees, coughing, he stares
At his gun, my badge.

He flops down, beaten.
"A fucking cop!" Strangled rage,
His mob armour smashed.

He hauls to his feet,
A sly sideways, whispered hiss,
"Be seeing ya!" threat.

I smile, "Bye, sweetheart."
He walks, glares back from the door,
Flips bird, night, rain, out.

I turn, look for her,

Not there, just the ugly crowd,

She is gone like smoke.

IV

So, I get the call,
Some dumb mug got 86'd,
And I head downtown.

Slow weave the traffic,
No rush, just another stiff
That's going nowhere.

I hit the sack late,
My head's full of last night, her,
Her look, her strangeness.

It'll pass, has to,
A world of ugly waits me,
She was beautiful.

Waterfront alley,
Uniform cops, "Fuck Off" tape,
Hacks taking photos.

"So, what we got here?"

"Hey Sergeant, you'll love this one!"

Slip under the tape.

He's face-down and stiff,

Yellow plaid and two-tone shoes,

Familiar it seems.

They spin him, I smile,

Frog-eyed, bluing face, tongue out,

It's him, the drunk hood.

"Have we got I.D.?"

"Nah, bill fold, switchblade, brass knucks"

"So not a priest then?"

"Holster but no gun"

"The killer took it maybe?"

It's safe in my car.

"Why leave the money?"

"Your guess is as good as mine."

"Disturbed?" "Yeah! Disturbed!"

"What's he been choked with?"
"Not wire or rope, skin's intact."
"Death put her gloves on!"

We stand up laughing,
He'll be swept up like the trash,
I think about her.

Back at the precinct,
I write up the strangled hood
From life to paper.

Think on what I know,
The asshole's last night on earth,
I hold those things back.

V

There's an old saying:
"What eyes don't see, heart craves not."
Well, too fucking late.

She had me hooked good,
She rattled doors I'd nailed shut
When the blonde left me.

I smelled something too,
My cop nose twitched like a cock.
Had she choked the hood?

So, I dog her close,
I catch her set a few times,
Hung back in the shade.

I like what she does,
Web spin over heaving beats,
A coy play of lace.

I trail her cab home,
And then again and again,
Gumshoe in a loop.

I thought I was smart,
Killers feel eyes like needles,
She knew, dumb fuck Cop.

VI

I wait in the rain,
Watching outside of her block,
Patient in the wet.

A cab pulls up sharp,
Hallway light, I hold in shade,
Her, I catch my breath.

Her eyes scan the street,
Feral under a slick brim,
I shade in the shade.

She slips liquid smooth,
Hauling that case big as her,
A cat with a kill.

Raincoat, ankles, in,
The door clumps shut into warmth,
Engine rev, she's gone.

The chorus of rain,

The tail-lights a distant fire,

I head to the door.

Generic hallways,

Her door, the lock gives easy,

I wait six heartbeats.

I open an inch,

The smell hooks, lines and sinkers,

What is this heaven?

I edge in, rapt, lost,

I nose deep in the thick swell,

This burst of other.

Heavy swirl of dope,

Flowers, blooms from God knows where,

So much incense, spice.

I friendly the dark,

Grab me some reality,

Make shapes in the night.

I focus, shape up,
Just remember why I'm here,
Cop head bursts the dream.

The room starts forming,
The gloom gives up its maybes
To cold dead knowing.

Her pad is bland, brown,
Like a thousand dull others,
Faceless as justice.

A sparse gleam passes,
The headlight picks a gilt glint,
Foreign in this drab.

Low table, dark wood,
On it a beautiful thing,
We're elsewhere again.

A bronze, a foot high,
Thumbed to gold by loving hands,
I feel jealousy.

A dancer, four arms,
Dark burlesque with a sickle,
Tongue out, lewd and fierce.

Scattered at the base,
Blood-red candy and flowers,
Gifts for a Goddess.

The bronze taunts my brain.
If this city has a God,
Then its name is fear.

Beyond the statue,
Her clothes and the crazy smell,
She was a ghost here.

I pause in the dark,
A softness brushes my throat,
Her weight hauls me back.

My hand touches silk,
I crash hard into her lithe,
Hear her breathe and yank.

Blood pounds in my head,
We thrash in the heat, she speaks,
soft, "Jai Ma Kali."

Elbow, fast, her ribs,
We both suck air, I claw silk
And she drags it tight.

I pull, breathe, rise up,
She clings to my back, kicking,
I bronco the room.

She swings, wood splinters,
Swirl of debris and incense,
This storm, no calm heart.

Ragged bebop air,
Fast breaths snatched in impact breaks,
Wild scat of her pain.

Bull the door, it gives,
My rider stays put, reins hard,
We spin in splinters.

I un-noose my hand,
She pulls, my eyes spin black stars,
Crawl, stair rail, I buck.

Wood cracks, she flips out,
Spins, dangling, still gripping silk
Over stairwell void.

I'm still reined, she jerks,
I choke and lock eyes with her,
Beautiful hatred.

I push up, one hand,
I reach in under my arm,
She knows, jerks again.

Salvation, my gun,
I aim it between her breasts,
She smiles, jerks, I fire.

She drops, a soft thud.
The silk slackens, I can breathe.
Slumped, hot broken man.

VII

She lies on the slab,
Nothing as still as the dead,
She is perfection.

Skin like white coffee,
Gentle marbling to her back,
Death's love bite creeping.

Her nipples lie flat,
Beyond cold, beyond passion,
Silent calm islands.

Her hair asphalt black,
A winter molasses spill
To the slab's steel edge.

Her smooth curves converge,
Draw the eyes unwilling down,
Compelled to her sex.

I think of her brain,
The muted machine of guts,
The if of her womb.

Half-parted lips, eyes,
Waiting for the Prince's kiss,
This beauty sleeps on.

There is but one flaw
In all this cold stone beauty,
A harsh screaming mar.

The black star-shaped hole
Where my bullet hit her chest
Hey! Nice shooting, Tex!

And then I feel it,
Like a fast right to my guts,
A hard summoning.

Inevitable,
As the ground is to a fall,
And I was falling.

I snatch a last glance,
Prowler eyes on her cold form,
I quit the death room.

I light up a smoke,
Breathe the question in my head,
So, what did I do?

VIII

It was a slow month
After I'd killed her, rain, wind,
The neck pains started.

We still had no name,
No one to tie her down to,
Except her victims.

The Jazz joints knew zilch,
"She came, she played and we paid.
Who needs a name, man?"

Her tally ran twelve,
Picked in ripe chunks from the files,
All choked, her M.O.

These dozen dead ones,
Picked from a sea of corpses,
Given a mother.

They stretched back a year,
Nothing similar before
And for sure not since.

Twelve no real losses,
As I scanned the files, I thought,
A crock of dead scum.

Two paedos, two pimps,
A slumlord and three hookers,
A rapist, three hoods.

The press ran with it,
She did our job with feeling,
Dubbed "The Jazz Angel."

Anyhow, my pain,
My neck was stiff from her hang
And didn't unstiff.

The mortis slid in,
A creeping grip up my skull,
A dead lover's hand.

Nights of ache-wracked sleep,
Awake to a harsh flurry,
Dream birds on the wing.

After the third day
Of steel wire tension torture,
I hit the doctors.

Bluff, bonding man stuff,
Sympathy for a tough guy,
Banter and smoking.

The big brass balls club,
Tell him the yarn, her killing,
Back slap, Scripts me dope.

Drug store done, my car,
Bottle open, swallow two,
Dry, white, bitter pills.

Turn the key, I pause,
I peel out and head southside,
To hers, for answers.

Inside her building,
Clean floor where she hit the deck,
Bloodless slab of tile.

The stairs up-circle
The down path of her plummet,
A vulture winging.

The landing, new wood,
Pine, varnish, smell of repair,
The heal of a breach.

Her room, door open,
Inside an old wooden crate,
"Can I help you, Mack?"

The building super,
I flash badge and he softens.
"Just following leads."

"All good, officer."
He smiles, I nod, "That her stuff?"
"All yours, help yourself."

I pick up the crate,

The pain barks loud in my neck,

"Thanks," I head downstairs.

IX

I start with a pill,
Because my neck is nagging,
Burdened by her corpse.

The pills are bedside,
They start the day and end it,
Numb up and numb down.

Roll my iron-stiff neck,
Pop and crackle like wood burn,
It becomes habit.

The precinct boys' joke,
"That bitch still hanging in there?"
Bone grind and laughter.

So, two becomes three,
The pills snug in the glove box
With my other gat.

And three becomes four,
Come on all wounded hero,
The quack ups my script.

My jacket rattles
With pain-killer percussion,
Dig that maraca!

Three pills become four
And five is no real number.
A bad day? One more.

So, five becomes six,
One more to help me slumber,
Prescribed, it's no fix.

The quack gets sniffy,
Eyebrow raised on my next ask,
I split, head downtown.

I park, a side street,
Ditch my tie and put on shades,
Blur my cop aura.

I find me a bar,
Nameless basement dive, perfect.
I take a beer, sit.

The back of the room,
A lean spade, sharp suit, good shoes,
As assured as God.

And paying sly court,
Furtive cherubs in sweaters,
Seeking his manna.

They sidle up slow,
Cool is the key to heaven
With this St Peter.

One wee whiff of square,
Even with a fold yay thick,
This dude will not sell.

Rumour his shingle,
His is the perfect product,
They beg, kill to buy.

The exchange is smooth,
A two-handed magic act,
Cash, dope, hey, presto!

No applause, no bows
And an audience of one,
A cop hid in shades.

Trade hits hiatus,
St. Peter stretches and splits,
I drift, his shadow.

My boy glides liquid,
Save for the cut of his suit,
He's invisible.

No pimp roll swagger,
This is one cool dope monger,
All go but no show.

I ghost him a block,
Hip to his cautious catting
This city's hot tin.

Unknown is what's next,
The bones, I will have his stash,
I mind-jam some scenes.

A straight buy won't wash,
That close up I'd stink of cop,
He'd know a mile off.

The same with a bust,
The bent cop gloms the goodies,
He'd finger me swift.

That leaves the strong arm,
Lead sap to the soft skull base,
They drop like a sack.

My boy takes a left,
My guess is to find his car
And what lies inside.

A plain black sedan,
It wouldn't raise an eyebrow
On fire in a crèche.

I shade the trash cans,
Waiting for the move moment,
He scopes, pops the trunk.

"Well hello, Lewis!"
My boy stiffens and turns slow,
I hunker down, watch.

The voice, a thin spick,
Upright rat on a diet,
In cheap seersucker.

His smile is golden,
A piece large in his rat hand,
Lewis, his lips hard.

"You been busy, man."
Lewis schtums, no point talking,
The game's up, he's bust.

Rat boy hoists the gun,
Smiles gold and pulls the trigger,
Brains spray the sedan.

I spring in raw hate,
Smash his face to the trunk lip,
He spits blood and gold.

I dive his pocket,
A switchblade, old street habits,
I ice pick his skull.

I scan the alley,
No eyes, I hear no sirens,
Willful, blind.

In the trunk my prize,
A dark tan leather suitcase,
Inside, junk heaven.

I trunk the rat's corpse
The blade jutting from his neck,
Lewis joins him there.

Trunk shut, pop the hood,
Fuel line off, gasoline spills,
Matchbook, womp and heat.

I quit the alley,
Find my car, stow the suitcase,
My cop mask back on.

So, I've crossed a line,
Heaven remains unfallen,
Consequence zero.

I wait for sirens,
I pull up, flashing blue lights,
Fire glow, uniforms.

Then the gas tank blows,
Burnt flesh wafts, I ask a cop,
"So, what's cooking, Mac?"

X

I stutter "Aw, gee!"
I'm the innocent abroad,
"I guess so, how much?"

She draws hard, "Twenty."
"Where?" She blows smoke at a rise,
Drops the butt, grinds it.

She swings slow ahead,
She sings a snatch of showtune,
Her voice some dead dream.

I follow her wake,
Cheap perfume, sweet, rotten blooms,
Cigarette smoke, booze.

Her skirt hugs the curves,
Stocking seams, worn fuck-me shoes,
A specter-thin blouse.

She leers back at me,
Wolf smile breaks through her lamb mask,
She turns and we walk.

We hit the darkness,
The coin in the scarf arcs fast,
She snags her last breath.

I drag her backwards,
Haltered with silk into shade,
She kicks at the brush.

She loses a shoe,
Painted toes through holed stockings,
Naked, embarrassed.

Throat sounds and thrashing,
Desperate nails claw at the choke,
Her eyes glaze and die.

I pocket the scarf,
I scope the park, voices waft,
Drop her the twenty.

Drunk act, tag a crowd,
Hide in the drift of others,
I sing a showtune.

XI

After the cookout
And firehose wash off my sins,
I hightail it home.

Home is a big word
For three rooms of brownest bland.
Who lives here? No one.

We married in June,
She still-birthed early April,
She left in July.

The radio, on,
A heady Jazz of lilies
In this dull charnel.

Three fingers of scotch,
I haul the case, pop the catch.
It's Christmas morning.

First the smell of tea
Heavy sweet, sticky, sickly,
I count eight small bags.

Then pills, ups and downs,
Ten of each in bags of ten,
Bad children's candy.

Then what I hoped for,
Neat white squares, ten wraps of horse
And fuck the pear tree.

Take one, stash the case,
The horse jams brown with the room,
Tone matched to numbness.

I empty a smoke,
Mix the tobacco with junk,
Reload the paper.

I hit the bedroom,
My neck aching, I lie down,
I spark and inhale.

The room spins, dissolves,
A tingling wave of pleasure
Caressing my skin.

Every ache, pain, gone.
Exhale, my tired flesh renewed,
Safe in the junk womb.

I toke, breath lifts me,
All is soft, cast in wonder,
Singular and warm.

Nausea rises,
Helpless slew of wheels on ice,
All control is lost.

I spew, the scotch burns,
Acrid liquid clash of drugs,
Choose whom ye shall serve.

I spit, flop back spent,
The retching subsides, I breathe,
All good, on the nod.

XII

When she got sweaty,
She had that unique blonde smell,
Honey and fresh bread.

Her dense secret hair,
Much coarser than a brunette's,
But so soft beneath.

The summer sun play,
Warming her writhe in gold shafts,
Her cunt, a halo.

XIII

A harsh, strangled gasp,
Brutal stir from submerged dreams,
Coffee calls, get up!

Head swim, brain chatter,
Sea leg waltz to the galley,
The jug, drown my sins.

Black flood, desert mouth,
Past best, lukewarm and bitter,
Mirrored, I stare up.

Cup two, the dead rise,
Lazarus sways to the lounge,
Pain and age check in.

The box, her dead things,
Touchstones to legal murder,
Memento mori.

I pull a silk scarf,
With it a burst of perfume,
Heady narrative.

The silk is weighted,
A coin sewn in its layers,
I spin it round my wrist.

A slick trick, lady!
They never saw how it's done,
I'd felt the magic.

A carved wooden box,
Inside, a small pipe, long stem,
Not smoking Luckies.

A nugget of tar,
Hashish? Opium? Sniff, both.
Old world holy dope.

Clothes from nowhere here,
Books in a script of the same,
Beneath these, the bronze.

I touch cold metal,
Skull garland and a full breast,
I put it all back.

I cold-dowse my face,
Shake off the fug of poppy
And head for a bar.

Dark corner table,
A smoke, three fingers of scotch,
The sane city drugs.

I glug for the burn,
Shroud up in tobacco wreaths,
But the numb don't come.

I can't lid this one,
She is everywhere, unseen,
The genie is out.

XIV

So, three glasses in
I find the brass cojones,
Face my own music.

So, what did I do?
I did what any cop would,
Shot a murderer.

The voice screams "Bullshit!
You killed something beautiful,
You motherfucker!"

I just did my job,
I protected this city,
Kept its people safe.

The voice screams "Bullshit!
You killed something beautiful,
You motherfucker!"

She was a killer,
Out of control, gone beyond,
I restored order.

The voice screams "Bullshit!
You killed something beautiful,
You motherfucker!"

I took out my piece
And put a thirty-eight slug
Through her beating heart.

I used lead justice
To smash the gold of her heart,
Twisted alchemy.

The fuck of my gun
Shot a warm, vibrant body
Into cold, dead meat.

I am the guilty,
I killed something beautiful
And so I must pay.

I upheld the law,
I did this for the city,
I am a dumb slave.

We are the city,
The ugly herd of people,
We are the guilty.

As she dropped, plugged, dead
She pulled off this city's mask,
I saw its true face.

XV

Under the neon,
It does her no real favours.
Who gets to choose light?

All beautiful things
In this city-long gutter
Are like ice in hell.

So, I watch her drink,
She's alone but who isn't?
I bide her time left.

She is close to spent,
Sucked dry by this hard city,
Taking on its hues,

She was pretty, once,
Some long years, some day ago.
Does she sense the end?

She takes a long slug,
Fuel for flight from her knowing,
Chipped nails through grey roots.

Time for my entrance,
Stand, walk, time the collision,
Hit her table hard.

She starts, ice rattles,
Teeth bared, fight/flight city eyes,
Lips move, "What the fuck?"

Smooth her with a line,
"Hey sister, sorry 'bout that!"
Smile, she softens, in.

"Getcha another?"
I resurrect her dead glass,
Liquid saviour.

So, I ply her need,
Keep the religion flowing,
Her numb sacrament.

Soft smile, listen close,
Everyone has a spiel here,
Me her confessor.

The usual story,
Love, loss, dreams that were stillborn,
Excuses for sins.

Nod, grin as required,
Strophing "I know what you mean."
Give her forgiveness.

The bar light halo,
Leeches her youth to the void,
Time her enemy.

We leave together,
I could be her rugged cross,
Her new salvation.

Desperate, enough,
An ear willing to listen,
This city's low hopes.

The streets empty now,
I slip an arm round her waist,
She sags a little.

Too much, drink, heartache,
Her perfume fails to hide it,
The musk of stale life.

She tastes of regrets,
Mouth to mouth in an alley,
Willing in the gloom.

She fails to notice,
My hands, the scarf, the kiss ends,
I speak, she listens.

An old woman dies,
We both leave for some elsewhere
In a state of grace.

XVI

So, I spin the dial
Into the outland white noise,
Far end of the wave.

Sift the static hiss,
Panning for the golden sound,
The Dead Beatnik Show.

This is the story,
Some junkie Jazzhead downtown
With a transmitter.

Fills the wee hours
With drug rap and hot bebop,
Outlaw Jazz cast broad.

A guy called Shorty,
Rambling wild on the night air,
Every cat digs it.

But not City Hall,
"A blot on our civic pride"
But we can't find him.

Worst of all, a fan,
Louelle, The Mayor's bad kid,
He smashes her set.

No one knows a thing,
The Mayor's now fit to burst,
Shorty gets wilder.

Believes his own spiel,
Ether flood of lewd and crude,
Jazz vignettes of filth.

"The Mayor fucks dogs
While the dogs eat chopped liver
Out of his wife's snatch!"

Uptown there's uproar,
Big pressures are brought to bear,
Things get real dirty.

We can't find Shorty
But we do find his dealer,
So, we make a deal.

The boy's choices are
Ten on a kiddy rape charge
Or he helps us out.

Next time Shorty scores
He dishes him a hot shot,
Closes down the show.

The boy can't argue,
Ten of bad food and ass fuck
Would persuade a rock.

So, Joe, the last show,
Word had slid out, as it does,
But not to Shorty.

He was too far out,
The heat, danger, junk and Jazz,
Mad elusive bird.

The Mayor threw a bash,
Invited all the slighted
To hear the swansong.

Glad hands and cocktails,
Centerpiece, a radio,
Big as a coffin.

Midnight from the hiss
Comes our man, high and live-oh,
Wired and yucking hard.

"Hey, alright, tonight!
We got a reeaaal special show!"
Uptown The Mayor smiles.

Shorty gabbles on,
But behind the riffs and rap
There is a giggle.

Shorty's not alone,
"So, say hello then Louelle!"
Uptown pricks its ears.

"Heeey!" A high, spoilt squeal,
"My daddy's the fucking Mayor!
He's a real asshole!"

Shorty and the kid
Dissolved in crazy laughter,
No one laughs uptown.

The Mayor grinds teeth,
"What you wanna do, Louelle?"
"Let's get high, Shorty!"

"Spoon and Miss Needle
Just love each other soooo much!
They can't get enough!"

Clarity's moment,
Fucked hard on their own petard,
The Mayor's wife screams.

They count down "Three, two"
He drops the stylus, crackle,
"One!" Both dead, bebop.

The platter spins on,
Catches a scratch and repeats,
A four-second loop.

And it does not stop,
No one can bury the dead,
They lie God knows where.

But the beat goes on,
Day three brings the buzz of flies,
Insect brass and fuzz.

The mayor retires
With his coffin-sized wireless
And his screaming wife.

Every junkie knows
Where to hear this city's pulse,
Out on the dial's edge.

Shorty's endless show,
A metronome to nod to,
And I have tuned in.

XVII

I'm loading her pipe,
Grazing from my drug buffet,
Tabled on corpses.

Barbequed Lewis
With rat on the side stay schtum,
Six lines in the press.

No one gives a fuck,
Two pushers get served up hot,
City licks its lips.

So back to the pipe,
I layer tea as a base,
Fragrant, resinous.

Then her soft hashish,
Chocolate dark, flame crumbled,
I lick my fingers.

I top with more tea,

A good pinch of horse to taste,

I'm ready to cook.

Spin the wireless dial,

Find the loop, gas mark Shorty,

My lungs are hungry.

XVIII

All things seek limit,
When they find their boundary
They cross it and change.

I skip the skin pop
And head straight for the mainline,
Needles in. Why not?

Through my day it's pills,
Light snacks for a screaming neck,
Come nightfall it feasts.

But this is a lie,
The real torture is elsewhere,
In my guts and soul.

I hide myself deep
In the sanctum of numbness,
But the walls, they creak.

I loose the leather,
The world comes apart softly,
Resolved and dissolved.

I exhale all form,
Each cell loses its tension
In calm liberty.

I float back in still,
Each breath paced at an aeon,
The void embraces.

Every atom comes,
This is the big petite mort,
Sex and death in waves.

I'm in utero,
A womb of poppy petals,
Junk amniosis.

My breath fossil-slow,
My lungs in tectonic shift,
I glacier-toke.

And then a tremble,
From out this dark comes a sound,
A screaming diamond.

The light hits me full,
The sound vibrates sheer panic,
I have got the fear.

The reverse of blind,
This pure luminous harshness,
I see too clearly.

I'm falling, light-speed,
Blind, deaf in the light and sound,
My scream jams off key.

Impact, cold and hard,
Broken, I'm a smear, a stain,
Bug on a windshield.

A string-cut puppet,
Ribbons of stark agony
Link my limp fragments.

And then she is there,
Her, but huge, God knows feet tall,
A cab foot stomps me.

Giant and naked,
Curves redrawn to landscape scale,
Colossus burlesqued.

Her skin night sky black,
Impossibly luminous
Against the hard light.

A whirl of ghost arms,
A sword cut from railroad track,
A cup to bathe in.

A leering hood's head,
Gripped by its greasy bouffant,
Wafts gore and cologne.

A double bed hand
Throws shapes and hidden message
With dance troupe fingers.

In this strange fairground
The sword and cup spin to hints
Of needle and spoon.

This ten-story broad,
She looms, a vertical shrine,
A sacred mountain.

My eyes crawl upward,
She grinds her foot, her thighs part,
Her quim like a grave.

My breath exits fast,
I am dirt between her toes,
Blood pounds, my head swims.

I stare up transfixed,
Her breasts, their vast perfection,
An earthquake made flesh.

I plead to her eyes,
Her smile frames a wound-red tongue,
The foot eases, I breathe.

She tilts her vast head,
In a voice like distant bombs
She asks the question.

"Tell me what you did?"
Her words hang like a storm front,
I wriggle in fear.

She allows me breath,
My cock twitches at her curves,
Zilch quells the small head.

"Tell me what you did?"
She flicks my face with her toe,
Sized like an armchair.

I taste blood, see stars,
Between her breasts a glow,
My guilt shot black hole.

I scream it out loud,
"I killed something beautiful!"
She smiles, cat sublime.

The foot goes, hands grip,
I'm hauled up to eye level,
A third burns her brows.

Her eyes locked on mine,
Slowly, she begins to sway,
The sway turns to dance.

She sings, who knows what?
Her voice a windswept forest
And nearing thunder.

A doll, I rise up,
In her grip and flail of arms,
A whirl of bare flesh.

I glimpse in her spin,
The night city laid in lights,
Her feet ghost the streets.

We wade through scrapers,
A bridge girdles her smooth waist,
Headlights jewel her sex.

All around this dance,
Through the city's brick carcass,
Corpse lights caress her.

Last sparks of the gone,
Blue embers of death's release,
She whirls and inhales.

She ceases her song
And holds me high in stillness,
Above this cold pyre.

Her voice lilts and rolls
"What do you see here, lawman?
What is it you serve?"

Below, a maelstrom.
"Show me your order, lawman,"
She gestures with me.

Seething in the grid,
The chaos of human life,
There is no pattern.

Unknowing below,
The thousands of lives and deaths
Play out to no one.

I see through my lie
To the only beauty here,
The stillness of death.

The story complete,
An end and then cool silence,
The light fandango.

I know the real law
And I know now whom I serve,
I know the beauty.

Praise be to Chaos
And praise be unto horror,
Praise be unto death!

She begins to laugh,
Her dancing becomes wilder,
I am whirled and spun.

She spreads three fingers,
I'm left noosed in an "OK,"
She tightens her grip.

The world spins, I scream,
Lights, curves, her laughter louder,
Everything goes black.

XIX

Heaven is white sheets
And it smells like hospital,
I guess I'm not dead.

That everything hurts
And my neck is braced says so.
Maybe this is hell?

"How you doin', son?"
It's Hagan, Chief of Police,
Not quite the devil.

"Don't you try and talk,
You messed yourself up real good."
I can't move or speak.

He steps into view,
"It's not permanent, you'll live"
Sounds like a sentence.

"Got some months here though,"
A stone slab in a grey suit,
Hat held by the pinch.

He stiffens, bad news,
"Your cop days are over though."
He stares, pity? Hate?

"Neighbours heard the noise,
Called it in, and we found you,
Damn as much near dead."

The rock's brow furrows,
"Stoned, nude, hanging from a door."
His hat is screaming.

"We cleared up your mess,
Called it a suicide try,
Hid all the damn drugs,"

"Kept the press away,
Turned the damn radio off!"
He hate-eyes the freak.

"You'll get your pension,
I fixed it, medical grounds,
But you're finished here."

"Our rep's bad enough
Without fucked up junkie cops,
Goodbye son, get lost!"

He turns on his heel,
His hat stops screaming, he leaves.
Why am I crying?

XX

The white hell drags on,
A repeated bad dream riff,
The horror of dull.

The meaningless clock,
I count the hours with pain,
Wake to ache to drugs.

Bland angels bring them,
Hairdos change from day to day,
But the starch white, not.

Each round is the same,
All is diminutive here,
"A little pill…. drink…."

They come with flat smiles,
I am Gulliver pain-bound
To little mercies.

They are uniform,
Name, age, voice all fuzz to "Nurse,"
A generic blur.

They are prim and clean,
They stir nothing within me,
For they are not her.

When I close my eyes
She is there in her vastness,
Havoc black and wild.

As Nurse bends near me,
The scent of antiseptic,
An anodyne fog.

But what my nose craves
Is her full animal stink,
Cunt, sweat, ass and blood.

Her powerful musk,
Battlefield and carnal bed,
Afterbirth and grave.

So, I am ruined,

By an impossible ache,

For a ghost, a corpse.

Mourning and guilty,

I killed something beautiful

And so, I must pay.

XXI

So, the weeks spin by
In the white, neuter Hades,
And I use my pain.

I work myself hard,
Lifting the weight of this world
With my screaming neck.

I learn to need pain,
I am defined by torment,
I refuse their drugs.

"Making good progress!"
God visits in a white coat,
Bestowing blessings.

He smiles and thumbs up,
Exits basking in the glow
Of my tortured cure.

I grow hard in hell,
Evolving from frame to stick,
From stick to the gym.

After six long weeks
I'm freed from the slave collar,
A hawk unhooded.

I hone my pain sharp,
The gym is mine all alone,
I scent-mark with sweat.

Nights leave me dream-wrecked,
Fucking with her in far space,
Wild stellar unions.

My cock a comet,
Her cunt a svelte nebula,
We fuck like Titans.

Atom to astral,
We come as the universe,
Wake in tears, human.

Grief and mortal ache,

Lover's balls for a dead girl,

Guilty killer's guts.

XXII

So, here's the big day,
God signs the discharge ticket,
Smile and thumb up, prick.

The bland angels wave,
Doors open into warm light,
The sick man is free.

XXIII

I am become love,
My eyes open in new ways,
I see my own sight.

I smoke in the heights,
The night city flows below,
The river, light, blood.

I still see her dance,
A fluid rainbow spectred
At my vision's edge.

From this view above,
My love for those souls below
Is overwhelming.

I sense the patterns,
The baroque bebop of life,
Entrances, exits.

I do so love it,

Its rhythm, strangeness, danger,

This is why I kill.

Of this penance, glad,

Of the world she has shown me,

She taught me to blow.

Death makes the spaces

So new sounds can wail the void

And the beat goes on.

I called her kills scum,

They were the unseen easy,

We fish the same pool.

So, search for reasons,

Beg for some morality,

Killers are lazy.

Balance the effort,

I can kill one president

Or a hundred schmucks.

You don't want to die?
Get lucky, get rich, be missed,
Suck that Karma tit.

Fame is for losers,
My art is invisible,
Seen only by her.

So, I'm heading south,
Toward feral heat and dust,
Drift, gig your cities.

Keep the riff rolling
For as long as I have breath,
Until you stop me.

I travel real light,
One suitcase, a thirty-eight,
The bronze from her pad.

I swing the coin weight,
Silk loop-nooses the rearview,
Dowsing for murder.

The bronze rides shotgun,

Throned on the passenger seat,

I am death's chauffeur.

The sky rumbles bass,

I flick my cigarette butt,

Fire arcs the darkness.

I start the engine,

Touch the cold, bronze curves for luck,

The rain starts again.

THE
GULLVEIG
WORKING

MY TAROT DECK rotates and coils in an onanist mitt and spills,

Dead men's business cards, losers' lottery tickets,

Un-redeemable pawn shop stubs for

Hearts and minds and souls,

Toe tags and thumb-smudged nudes, traitor's fingerprints

And cigarette cards for the hundred greatest

Cancer-killed poets.

These jailhouse-scavenged pocket scrapes and detritus

Shower a floor not worth killing for

With an unhappy confetti,

Spelling murder and fear in its disarrayed entrail tumble

On to bare boards.

And the solid truth is I am the hungry dead,

Dragged, drugged and Draugred,

And in my revenance I'll chase mystery all over this damn town,

Like she was a blonde in a red velvet dress,

All curves and lips and promises.

And this corpse I have become will spin the whispers

From the traffic hum and eavesdropped cold cuts of conversation

As I carve through the crowd on an aimless trajectory.

DERIVE-UH!

And I'll gaze long into the shew stone of a dead mobile

For a glimpse of the next empire

And hope for the Queens ear.

John DEE-REEVE-UH!

In these sub-savage streets

And pseudo-strange days,

Where the red rivers of Powell

Are the only Enochian

And I am Peeping Tom

For the Godiva cadaver of this prurient world,

Tied dead in the saddle of the palest of horses.

DERIVE-UH!

All geographies are psycho regardless of the situation and its isms.

On a pavement sift I'll ponder the spew of a spilled night,

Auger the patterns for some glimpse

Abroad the cities' palimpsest dreams,

Haunt the drinker's trails across this place,

See it rainbowfracted in the dripping prism

Of the spittle on a pisshead's chin,

Tracker on the hunt,

Urge within for buckskins and a Bowie

And a hat with a brim

To cast a shadow over my own dark,

A place to hide.

DERIVE-UH!

DERIVE-UH-HUH!

DERIVE-UH!

DERIVE-UH-HUH!

It becomes an Elvis mantra,

I can't remember a day

Without I saw The King's face or heard his name,

And let's take a trip on that name

Elvis — he is EL-VIS,

He is Elf Wisdom,

AL-VIS – he is all wise!

Just how many eyes behind

Those steering wheel shades?

"There is but one King"

And it is awakeness!

And I, this wounded corpse,

Splash TCB

On my Presley stigmata.

Oh heal me King of Kings

Of this King's evil!

Woe for I have to judge my heart

Against your brilliant feather,

But you and I know it weighs like a lead tombstone

And I am found eternally wanting,

For Lo The Tupelo Midas spins

Base vinyl into gold!

The King looms carbohydrate large,

The shadow of his own light cast

As he discorporates and becomes

"EVER-MORE!"

Thus quoth the raven-haired

Jumpsuit sparkle regent,

Tired of this guise he lets out a laugh—

"There is only one eye in King"—

And is gone, leaving me alone

In the clamour of his

Own-Din.

And I'm still dead.

And aching for mystery.

So maybe she's bored with my hounding,

Maybe it's a reward,

She won't tell me,

That broad in the red velvet dress

Is elusive beyond Elysian

And I'll claw my way through concrete

For a hint of a whisper of a rumour

Of her perfume

In a room she thought about going into

Once a thousand lifetimes back

When I was still hint and dust and starlight.

So Madame Mystery

Sends a sister

And she's sweet and says her name is Gullveig

But she prefers Goldslut or Goldie

And I like that

And we talk and I dig her

And her fire and her need

And she turns me on

To her junk

And her junk is GOLD

And she tells me it's called awakeness

But it's junk and it's Gold

And she doesn't even have to push.

So I ask her, "Where do we score this?"

And smiling she says, "Babe, the streets are paved with gold."

So she drives me crazy with lust,

For gold, that is.

Your other passions fall witch tit flat

In the face of this fever.

But let's interject about that other junk

For the squares,

So they have a hint of that hit and can dig something

Out of this diahorrea of a madman.

It's the whole thing,

The needle, tourniquet etc, etc,

The ache like waiting to inhale

And then

A birth pain,

A tingled flood of pleasure,

Pure,

Tied to Nothing

Or anything better,

Pulling six aces on orgasm,

The grand "Fuck it!"

In that lengthened breath,

The release from all mortal pain,

The perfect instant

In the cease of then and when,

The notion of a power to breathe

The whole universe

In lungs like angel wings,

The feel of things long hidden found again

In dream remnants,

The paradox and wonder

Of being made of lead, light and helium,

The absence of hate

Even for myself,

The forgiveness, the forgiveness, the forgiveness,

The sink into the burning cool

Of an angel kiss to the forehead,

Like a bullet made of your own laughter,

The universal dark behind your closed eyes,

The wonder of this secret vibrating stillness

Rich with the sound of void,

The nausea, satiety and hunger,

The plunge of awakeness into sleep.

In that sleep dive into dreams,

This is love.

And I'm back out searching and I'm alive-alive-oh.

Sold to Whittington's lie

By Goldie with her cat eyes and curves,

I'm dead again but don't know it.

Nothing beats that glint in the dirt,

The swoop, the cold feel of the metal,

The certainty of a score.

I am possessed,

I am nothing without it,

I am beyond why's.

You see the trails and tracks

In every street, gutter and drain

And sift for Sif within,

I can smell the pools of loss,

I follow the armies of fuck and fight,

I Raven and wolf in their wake,

Shark frenzied at a drop of the red gold in the water,

I start seeing the sense in cutting

The Christ-chained throats of those fools

And in biting those fat besovereigned fingers off,

It's wasted on them, wasted on them!

Can't they see it?

Just give it up, you fuckers!

THE PRECIOUSSSSSSSS!

But I hush myself and play by the rules.

The real map of any city

Is a Rorschach in blood
Scrawled by a lunatic
With a spirograph
Made from his own pelvis.
So I walk the rice paper of blood and lust,
Of random violence,
For the gilded sheddings and splinters
Of accident,
The spill from perceived slights,
From drugs and King alcohol,
The sweepings from Dionysus's weekend night reign,
He rules, his libations
Wash away all pain,
And I sift his drift and pan
For the earrings, rings and bangles and things
With an eye ever open for the glister.
And that eye is sharp
For the venues of fuck and fight,
The illicit places,
The culvert and backway,
The uncivil spaces outside of time,
Jotunheim down an alley,
Arenas for fucks that bring no life
And fights that fall short of death,
All that energy spilled and circling,
Undissipated in a whirl of frustration,

Seeping into the brick and concrete
Like rain.
And that seep can tension a city,
Bring it to a blood heat and on
Until it all boils over and King Riot reigns!
Or more likely the tension gives
And the town goes slack, reality loses elastic
And everything sags
Into the dull grey wash of unfulfillment,
The myth of renewal is broken
And if the myth dies
The city becomes undead, revenant, artless.
All things must fuck and die to live.
Magpie-eyed and seething with the need,
I stalk the gutters,
Bugged by the gold, a Poe-fevered ache and ague,
I cop glimpses in this mania,
This human obsession,
Gold, Gold, Gold,
And I see in those slices
A junk history, laid out in cadaverous avarice
As my eyes hawk the ground
For the slimmest glimmer.
And Burroughs's junkie question
Hangs cock-heavy, corpse-limpid and stinking:
"Wouldn't you?"

You know you would.

I see it shine on a thousand throats

And fingers and ears

And I covet, covet, covet

But I can't steal,

The rules of her game,

Finders keepers only,

Augury from the curlicues of unreadable signets

That send you hither to a likely seam.

So carrion-clad I track the trails'

Violence, loss and happenstance,

New roads for fresh kills in an old town,

Following the animals,

From watering hole to where they clash to where they fuck,

Vulturing the desert-strange ways across

In hope of scraps.

The Words Of The Very High One

I know I was strung out

Four score years and some

On the windy streets

Wounded by the needle

Junkie Bill given to Old Bull Lee

On those streets of Interzone

Where Nova Mob knows

From what party they rise

They dealt me no bug powder, no Mugwump jism,
Staring down at my shoe
I spied a vein,
Screaming, I spiked it,
And fell back on the nod.

But I digress, eternally,
So on you pan, you miner sixty-niner,
Forever after the Goldrush,
Pan the city's culverts and kneel you in,
They are its filthy veins and bowels,
And your eyes down for the Bingo of the glint,
So tell me true, on the rack, wrack of your obsession,
You spin your eyes gutterward for the merest hint of a glint,
Enthralled at a toffee wrapper,
Hard on for a ring pull,
It's hardwired within you now,
The most hopeful man in town, he looks for gold in the shit,
Gaze up and blind in the sun and it is gold,
Eyes down and blind to all else save that glint
And the heart skip
As you pan on and on
On the cities' hidden tracks of fuck and fight,
For the cursed Rhinegeld, you Alberich, you Uber-prick,
Mired in the midden

Of others' loss, bad luck and tough fucking shit.

She is in that glint.

Like the shooting star flash

Of gusset in the cross of legs,

In that Silbury white mound of breast,

In a view through liberty-straining buttons,

The raptor eye plummets headlong, into the valley

Of cleavage, cleavage, cleavage,

Like the satori distraction of a bitten lip

Or a sideways glance through lashes,

The back drag on a wave caught just right,

She is beauty

And the promise of a love supreme.

She is in every curve

And every cunt and mouth

You've known,

But more in the ones you never have or will.

She is whore and virgin,

She is Old Crowley's doubt

And he was always in debt.

And you would pass up

Any booze, junk or cunt

For this golden whore and her locks,

She is just right,

For she is the thing that is better

Round every corner of every block

And she is the grass that is greener
And the prophet who makes it so,
She is just right,
And she promises the world
And everything in it
And you know this lie is her truth
Because all are under her spell
And none can resist her smile
Or promise of her fix.
But especially not you,
Oh grubber in the dirt and shit and gutters,
And you would burst your heart asunder,
Olympiad of the sewers,
With your eyes on the golden prize,
So on and on but there is no finish line for thee.
The Tarot begins with you, oh fool!
And your optimism and its junk blindness,
Hope is the monkey on your back.
And wouldn't the world
Twist beauty-full if we all dug just the one agree
On a single thing?
And wouldn't peace be the thing,
And we all not brothers and sisters be
In a unity rapturous, harmonious and endless?
Well here's the news, suckers,
We do!

We agree on her worth and beauty

And our junkie need,

And every day is a kill spree

In her name

Because of our togetherness!

Halle-fucking-lujah!

And you can hear her laughter

Rattle within every final choking breath

As she pulls the pin on another Golden apple

And lets it roll baby roll

Into the heart of our own avarice, pride and delusion.

And the real mystery

Is our fascination,

What is this madness?

It's not just its hypno-pretty glint, surely?

What is this madness?

Dying Poe reaches out,

Touches the angel Gold Bug and expires,

What is this madness?

We irrationalise our guilt,

Flee whole hog into

Annunaki, miner slave fables,

Seek otherworld absolutions,

Alienate ourselves from the guilt

Of madness and obsession,

Cover it over,

But still it slumbers

Safe as the standard

By which it is the measure of all things,

This lust the dragon on the hoard

Of our occupied consciousness.

Oh little yellow metal,

Who made thee?

Was thou birthed in the heart of a burning sun?

Was thou the shit of the Gods,

As the Aztec heart rippers surmised,

With their priest fists full of gore and pumping meat?

Thou marks our bonds

And rings a world of bonded fingers

And sly the message to the metal bonded,

This the love enduring.

Thou drinkest deep of the meaning

Of all you touch,

Thou pretty vampire of value,

The Rhinegold taint is the blood in your veins,

The red gold is bloodied

And beyond all earthly defeat

For there it lives not.

Thou hidest behind an innocence false,

Thou whore of whores,

Thou virgin of virgins

Who is all promises.

Andst we give to thee

Who is perfect and reproachless,

Unsullied even steeped in the blood

Of numberless horrors wrought in thy name.

Butter-soft and harmless,

You ever fresh and willing malleable,

Blameless as a child at crib,

But it is we who are molded,

Called quicker to action than a babe's cries could summon

By this, the changeling fair.

Uncorrupted, uncorruptable

And yet the spur to all corruption,

And we'd crawl a million squelching miles

Over a charnel field of our own dead infants

For one of your smiles

Our MAAAAAAMMOOOONNNYYY!

Christostomos opens Ulysses

With a smile and a razor

And he knew history was a nightmare

He was trying to awake from

And we know the horror

Of death camp forceps.

Is it safe?

And of slavery and a sea of Inca blood,

So try not to think about

Where the smile glinted

Before it graced that loved one's knuckle,

Gold-fingered into that eternal Bond,

But it's there

In its gold DNA, in its blood,

Its history, its myth,

For this is where she lives, Goldie!

So deny the tiny human horror,

And as you stare into the glint,

Behold! In that gilded smile,

The face of a monster,

Oh Caliban enraged!

So we Rune that we begin with a fee,

There are no free rides,

And we begin with a lie,

That cattle are gold,

But we are the cattle,

Everything lies,

All is symbol, a glyph, a cipher,

A hint at some mystery,

A clue in this case,

In which you are the cop,

The corpse, the murderer, the witness,

The whole damn pack,

And you are worse than all liars,

You are lies.

And behold it gives us absolution

From the pain of thinking, like all junk,

And it is not evil

But we are for our love of it,

And it is a hope

Of all salvation

And a lie,

And we forgive it

All our trespasses,

And pray that God

Is golden

And make him over

In gold

In hope of ab-solvo-lution

But it is all a lie.

I was torn from earth,

I was a coin,

I was an idol,

I was a crown,

I was a cross at a slit throat,

I was a tooth,

I was stolen,

I was stolen,

I was stolen,

I flowed to your hand

On a river of blood and atrocity

And you will forgive me
And you will believe
The lie that you tell yourself
That I am as the lamb,
Innocent.
But for every lamb
There is a tiger,
And you have seen her
Ride it in Schleswig,
And you have seen her
Straddle the besom
And been jealous of that stick
And apprenticed yourself
To her source, sauce and sorcery,
So tell me her need
Was gold anymore,
Riding the tiger,
A millennia before Evola cribbed
And the sad old men with their flaccid staffs
Turned her golden LOVE to EVOL
And I am a Gilded Master
So you have to dig my truths!
And if you sup from that crock of shit
You'll never be one!
And you'll need a cat's cradle of Valknots
To ladder you out

Of the grave

Of your sorry belief.

And you realise this shit

Was just in your head.

Well fuck you, Alice, with your golden locks,

We love you

And the creations of Carroll's

Be they Lewis, Christmas or Pete,

That it's all just

Cold, Frankenstein and murder

And you know that to posses

Is to become a possession

And you empty your pockets

And having nothing

There is nothing

And you gain everything

And you stalk the dead roads

For the Buddha

With a twelve-inch bladed Bowie

You bought from Old Bull lee

And you made this happen,

And it's all junk

And you are the prophet

Who makes the grass green

And you made the gold golden

And all the blood is on your hands.

And your eyes spill like dice

Across the dirt of this town

And you're eternally trying your luck in the filth,

Let it roll baby roll, all night long,

And the wager is your sanity,

Snake eyes, sevens, pairs and elevens,

And you are The Diceman,

What's in a name

Luke Rhinehart

And what's the heart of the Rhine if it's not gold?

And Luke begat Look and luck

But it's all low-key

And you see his huckster eye behind

A fucked up scheme like this,

And you've met her too,

The Maiden of all Rhinemaidens,

You saw her in a hashish reverie,

The woman with a thousand dice for a head,

She is Chaos, she is Runa,

She is all faces and none

As you long for that one you've never seen,

So Hugin and Muninn

Magpie up in a small white lie

And become dice and the halves of your fevered brain

And there is fear as they tumble abroad

The green baize of the worlds.

So I'm slapped in the midnight line at a central Station convenience (so called) with the un-waiflike waifs and not strayed far enough strays, all seeking further oblivion in the first minutes of a new day. I need some wine and bread for a less than holy communion with inebriation and satiation, my eyes are on the ground despite Oscar's wild advice regarding stars, because drunk, sober, asleep or awake I'm still mania-ed maenad and panning and panting for gold in the Klondike of this gutter. I also shoe gaze because the last thing I need or want is a conversation here, my reality does not interface, it doesn't play well with others. A heavy set, dirty (on several levels) blond with a boxer's nose and more freckles than skin has just flashed her tits to the acne-riddled boy dispensing numbness at the hatch, perhaps the mutual speckling confused her, tripped her into this blatant mating rite, she's laughing harsh and cigaretted, she cops her lager and smokes and slumps off into the night with an equal punchy pulchritudy friend.

I should dish the skinny on the hatch it seems. The goods are slipped through the said hatch at this hour, the corporate paranoia of robbery and rank incivility looming large in a gamble against profits from the almost blind drunk. So I'm ground-watching, waiting my turn when I catch a glint! There before me, a yard away is a gold ring. I quit my place in the line in a heartbeat, this score beats any ten minutes more in homage to the hatch. The ring is thin and cheap and is set with a black stone heart, the metaphor to the town is blatant and coarse but it's gold and it's all the damn world in that instant, rapt and elated and greedy I scan further and there shining on the pavement is a pool of blood, its colour muted in the sodium to an inky limpid, I step up and the carrion man Narcissuses a death's head into the black, I scope for more horror in this show, oh my brothers and Droogs, and there it is: a scalp-torn tuft of bottle-auburn hair.

The whole sorry scenario plays out in the myriad scenes and minutiae of this butcher-fresh brute encounter. Whose ring? Whose blood? Whose hair? Who did what and why? Was it a him, another her? Come on, Gumshoe! There was sex afoot in this game and sheer luck saw you here to witness this graphic passion play left in sordid haiku on the pavement, Ripperesque grand guignol leavings on a lonely drunken corner.

And this I know is the last fix, the final piece of this puzzle, a blood full stop before my heart turns stony black to match, this is the last gold.

And I tell you, Oh seeker
Of this mania,
Not as warning
But as a necessity like water.
So now you have your snatch of gelt
And you spill the shrapnel of grenaded hopes and dreams
Through your avariced carrion fingers
And savour the heartache
Of loss and broken hearts and betrayals

And the million things this gold has been

Of the glinting magick fragments in Welsh streams,

And the hidden hoards as yet unfound

And you know that as the owners bled out

With futile fingers to spilled guts and blood

That their last thought wasn't home or cunt or mother or the Gods

But that gleaming heap they'd never see again,

Of the slog and slavery in the African mines,

Of the Spanish slaughter,

And the gilded mouths and Jew gold and theft

And the coins, the coins

And the thousand, thousand hands

That have touched it and the desire

Of every eye that beheld

And you trickle all human history through your fingers

And you are as much this gold as it is your story.

So you have your stash and you're burned out

And used up by it and the search

And The Blonde and her just right urgings.

And the mania is salved by this brief cool satiation

And you think as you finger your pile of murder

"Well what the fuck now?"

And in that instant

The note flutters down from the ceiling

In a shower of Golden sparkles and a whiff of snatch and perfume
And it's from Her:
"Sorry Babe, had to split town, Ciao. Goldie XXX"
And you're alone again
With a fistful and broken promises and an ache
For curves that are gone, gone, gone
And you're coming down faster than fucking Daedalus
From this trip,
Awake from the mania.
So you trek a careful cat's path
Over this, the ice
Of your abandon.
Eyes up, Motherfucker!
You're not grubbing in the dirt,
That game's over, you sap!
But your treacherous heart still flickers
At a glint
Wherever it may be
Fingers, ears, throats
And cleavage, cleavage, cleavage
In an incessant gilded incendiary echo.

So you gather your indecision and stash the gilt
Under the bed with the weapons and secrets and porn and dust
And you incubate like an old Greek
On a goatskin,

Seeking a salve for the cold turkey of an ordinary life,

Hide your panic

In something Pan-ic

Daddio. Dio IO! IO! IO!

And hope in some dream that comes

You'll find the next thing and ease.

You let that pony run,

Maybe all gestation is a nine-month,

You dragon your hoard,

Snug up on the pillow

Of your holy avarice

Awaiting the voice of the Dragonish guest

That is your own awakeness

And its word and sword

That slays you for the third time,

Oh thrice-dead Gullveigman,

And drives your serpent inertia OUT! OUT! OUT!

Into action

As the creative destruction surge

Splits the seed in growth

And spirals on the axis of your imagination.

Sleep, baby, sleep.

And the gold cold turkey is over

And waking on this dawn of all days

You want beauty about you

Like a blanket on a cold one.
So the gold is yours to use,
This is your prize for slaying the dragon
And the blonde is gone
But there's always another.

So your instinct is to bin the junk,
Cash it in on a wild night out, Give yourself an occult yarn to spin
About how you dumped the gelt
In a lake or a river or a bog
Knowing full well that riff will run like a sore,
The stash growing cock-like with every retelling
Till the legend wets the lips and loins and soaks some to the skin,
Popeyed with the Tsetse bite of the bug
In search for your lost gold.
But you won this glittering mittful of the sun
From the jaws of madness herself,
Caught that lunatic dose,
The gold Junk Pox
And flogged yourself three times deceased
Oh Herpes Trismi-dead–horse.
You died in that moment
When your eyes opened and
You saw that all was dead,
Including you,
Your love was dead to this world

And your second death was your will,

Dead to all else but

The search and the mania and lust for her

And your final death was even that

And thus the world came back to you alive

And knew that all you were,

Were love and will.

So you give nix to that

In the dark Nox of this comedown

And hang on to your souvenir loot

And thinking hard with your one eye closed

And stood on one leg

You glom the notion to giveth this thing

That was yourself in the long months of madness

To yourself.

This glint that was the whiphand

That became who you were,

That began where you ended and blended

And vice-versa

Like all great loves,

Of this thing you are now the master,

It lies under the thumb of your will.

You've seen the blood and pain of it

And know she is a great servant,

Makes Mercury for a sluggard

And can buy all the steel and lead,

But she the worst of mistresses

Because you give it all up for that love supreme,

All control

And as Old Bill glommed,

What does control want?

More control.

But this is the oldest yarn,

We awake and seek power and fall

From that infantile, innocent grace.

Go find yourself a smith

(If you can smith for yourself well bully [Bull Lee],

Some of us can only bend words to our will),

And you get him to dwarf you up your beast

In this gold of yours,

Maybe get him to spill a vial of your blood and mead

Into the mix

But you are the Master Oh Gullveigman

And the rules writ here are yours alone

But make it beautiful,

Make it so your heart leaps

At each glimpse and touch

As your breath draws in,

As you peek in the pouch,

So give yourself this beautiful thing,

Bind it into your power,

Now the glint serves your need,

Can carry,

Can Fetch.

And make them all jealous

That your eyes don't shine

Like that at them

And smile, Oh Master,

For you know it and this world are mere glyph and seven veils,

That your idol is not The Golden Calf,

It is not the blonde in any fucking red dress,

It is yourself,

Your one true love,

The spark of you

That is eternal awakeness,

Glowing warm and dancing wild

In the light

Of its own dark fire.

D. Jonathan Jones

December the nineteenth 2015

David Jonathan Jones
can be contacted through the publisher.

Made in the USA
Middletown, DE
25 June 2019